Mapping SEN

Mapping SEN

Routes through identification to intervention

Amanda Kirby

 David Fulton Publishers

This edition reprinted 2006 by Routledge
2 Park Square, Milton Park, Abingdon, Oxon, OX14 4RN
Simultaneously published in the USA and Canada
By Routledge
270 Madison Avenue, New York, NY 10016

10 9 8 7 6 5 4 3 2

British Library Cataloguing in Publication Data
A catalogue record for this book is available from the British Library

ISBN 1 84312 460 2

Typeset by FiSH Books, Enfield, Middx.
Printed and bound in Great Britain

MAPPING SEN: *routes through identification to intervention*

ILLUSTRATIONS

Figure

INTRODUCTION

Mapping SEN provides SENCos, teachers and teaching assistants with a means of identifying and meeting pupils' special educational needs. The program shows how children can be 'looked at' in a number of ways to understand why they behave in a certain way and what may be the cause of a difficulty, and then what strategies can be tried.

It allows the teacher or classroom assistant to observe the child and identify the (often overlapping) signs of difficulty and then provide a practical approach to helping the child. At the same time the indicators may allow the teacher to see if further assessment is required.

Sometimes children are given labels that do not always help the teacher to know how to support that child effectively. One child with dyslexia will be different from another. A child with ADHD may also have problems with reading and writing. The label alone does not give the answers. In order to meet the needs of the child, a tailored and functional approach is needed.

To be able to provide this, it is important to assess all areas of learning and to see which areas need to be addressed (the different components for learning). It is also useful to look at different behaviours and see what has triggered them and what this may then indicate.

Mapping SEN shows a number of reasons for different behaviours and then allows the user to see if patterns are developing and whether the individual 'symptoms' may actually be part of a cluster of indicators for underlying causes – such as motor difficulty or visual processing difficulty. This then

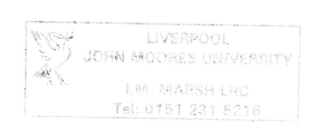

leads to a fact-finding mission in order to piece together the jigsaw and understand more about the causes of various difficulties.

Mapping SEN starts to take the teacher or learning support assistant along this process and suggests strategies to try.

The book and CD provide:
- An analysis tool for mapping individual needs
- Photocopiable record and assessment sheets
- Immediate access to straightforward information about a variety of special needs
- Approaches and strategies to help you to develop personalised support for pupils

This is a must have resource for every school that is serious about inclusion.

chapter 1

USING THE PROGRAM

SIGNS AND STRATEGIES IN THE CLASSROOM

SPECIFIC LEARNING DIFFICULTIES

MANAGEMENT

COMPONENTS OR ROUTES FOR LEARNING

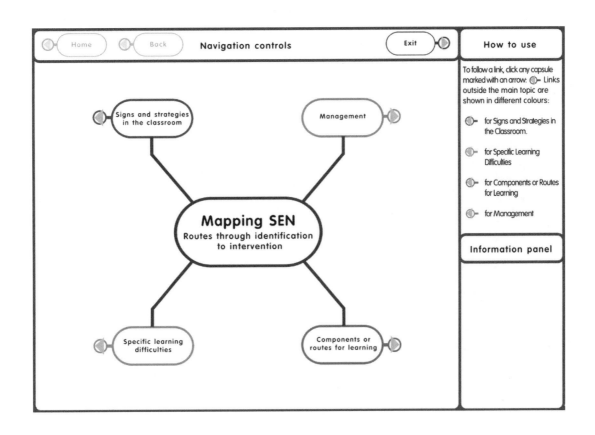

Mapping SEN can take you in four main directions:

1 What do you see? *Signs* in the classroom *and strategies* to help
2 *Specific learning difficulties* – what are they?
3 *Management* – issues to consider within the organisation to support the learning processes.
4 *Components or routes for learning* – what causes difficulties?

From each starting point, the program opens up further and allows the user to work through the different stages.

Every screen has the opportunity to take the user back to the **Home** page There are also **back** arrows

that takes the user back to the previous page.
The **How to use** panel remains on screen whilst the user navigates around the program and provides a key to the colour coding for the links on the screen. Text will appear in the **Information panel** when the user rolls over a capsule and further information links to that capsule.

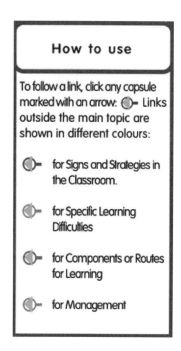

SIGNS AND STRATEGIES IN THE CLASSROOM

You may like to try this test run:
Click on **Signs and strategies in the classroom** and open this screen:

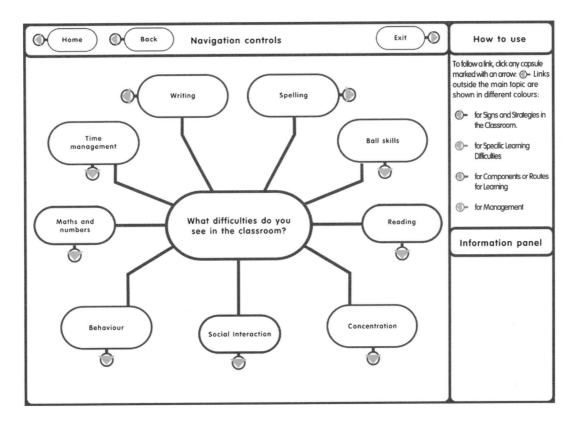

Click on the **Behaviour** box to open a screen which gives an overview of circumstances that can affect a pupil's behaviour. Some of these areas link to further screens (e.g. **ADHD**). If you click on the box, a new screen will open showing other 'symptoms' associated with ADHD. (Click on the back button to return.)

From Signs and strategies in the classroom, click on the **Behaviour** link.

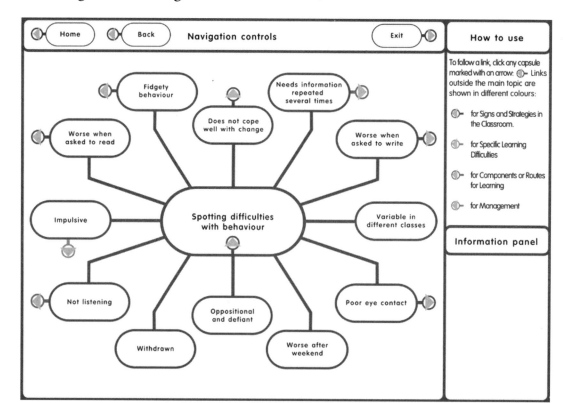

From here, click on **Difficulties with behaviour** to see all the ways in which behavioural difficulties can present in the classroom. Clicking on the boxes on this screen may open a sentence in the **Information panel** on the screen or take you to a new/interconnected screen. For example, if you click on **Does not cope well with change**, it will take you to the **Social and communication difficulties** screen. If you click on **Worse when asked to write** it will take you to the **Difficulties with writing** screen. (Click on the **back** button to return.)

SPECIFIC LEARNING DIFFICULTIES

Returning to the **Home page** allows you to click on **Specific learning difficulties** which leads to a list of SpLDs:

- ADHD
- Asperger's syndrome
- Developmental co-ordination disorder (dyspraxia)

- Dyscalculia
- Dysgraphia
- Dyslexia

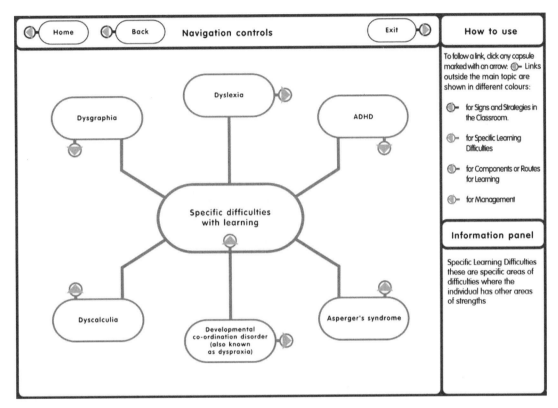

Clicking on any of these opens up a new screen with details about how to identify particular types of difficulty.

MANAGEMENT

Returning to the **Home** page allows you to select **Management** which leads you through all of the issues associated with managing SEN provision:

- Inclusive practice
- Assessment
- Intervention
- Support
- Process.

Clicking on any of these categories will open up a new screen with further information. With SENDA (Special Educational Needs Disability Act) being enforced, the need not only to recognise but to support adequately is now essential. The Management level in the CD-ROM shows strategies to ensure reasonable adjustments are considered and may be started even while perhaps waiting for further assessment.

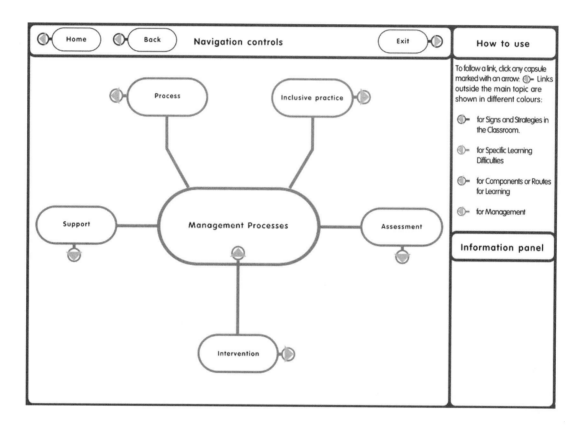

COMPONENTS OR ROUTES FOR LEARNING

Returning to the **Home** page now allows you to select **Components or routes for learning**, which opens a screen showing all the processes that are fundamental to learning (e.g. motor skills). It highlights the need to look at the whole child rather than at one 'weakness' in isolation. Clicking on **Motor** opens up a further screen with more detail.

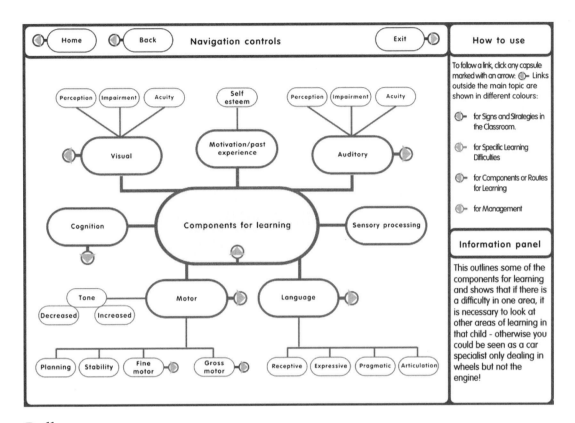

Roll mouse over text

This will highlight a particular box – some words may appear in the Information panel with further explanation.

Single click

This will move you on to a link on another page, if there is one there – this is indicated as a coloured arrow linked to the box.

chapter 2

DIFFICULTIES THAT CHILDREN EXPERIENCE IN THE CLASSROOM

SPECIFIC LEARNING DIFFICULTIES

Children may present with various difficulties in the classroom but may not be identified (labelled) as being 'dyslexic', 'dyspraxic' and so on. The main areas of difficulty are:

- **General difficulties:** Organisation, time management, adaptability, self-help skills, not always able to express ideas in writing, difficulty with orientation in a new environment, difficulty copying from the board (taking down homework), getting tired more easily than peers.
- **Literacy-based difficulties:** Reading, spelling, recording, writing with meaning, understanding new material.
- **Numeracy-based difficulties:** Number difficulties, problems with calculations (especially at speed), geometry and times tables, difficulty remembering a sequence of numbers.
- **Co-ordination-based difficulties:** Sequencing tasks, putting together tools and equipment, completing tasks to time and with accuracy, running and negotiating space, recording difficulties, undertaking tasks at speed, team-based sports.
- **Communication-based difficulties:** Team-playing, understanding commands, literal interpretation of instructions, understanding rules, poor social interaction, interrupting others, lack of empathy, social isolation.
- **Attention difficulties:** Impulsiveness, lack of concentration, difficulties staying on task, fidgety, lack of focus, answering out of turn.

Increasingly, however, children are identified as having certain types of difficulty which suggest a specific condition such as:

- Dyslexia
- Dyscalculia
- ADHD
- DCD (developmental co-ordination difficulty)
- Asperger's syndrome.

These are often referred to as *specific learning difficulties* (sometimes SpLDs).

SPECIFIC LEARNING DIFFICULTIES

Specific learning difficulties affect up to ten per cent of the population, many of whom have an average or above-average IQ. Many of these children have more than one area of difficulty.

Diagnosis may be made by different professionals using different assessment methods and then used to assign 'labels' to children – often as a way of securing extra support at school. Some are diagnostic labels but some are behavioural labels.

There are no simple 'cures' for these difficulties as there are many different causes, and each child has been exposed to a different environment and a different family setting.

Common threads of individuals with specific learning difficulties:

- More males than females are usually recognised in the school years; females may present later.
- Each child may present with different difficulties due to overlap with one area and another.
- Some children may not have difficulties until later, such as in secondary school when tasks have to be done faster.
- Problems often occur for the child when there is a choice of speed or accuracy and the child may have to make that choice.
- The child may have difficulties when expected to multi-task.

It is important to recognise the difficulties in order to:

- Acknowledge for the individual that the difficulties are real.
- Prevent discrimination by others.
- Reduce the risk of low self-esteem in the child.
- Reduce the risk of litigation because of non-compliance with the disability discrimination act and SENDA.
- Ensure there is appropriate provision of support.
- Consider training needs of the organisation and the staff within it.

- Consider the alternative approaches for teaching support.
- Share in best practice in supporting individuals.
- Consider approaches to integrate the child into the context of health, social and educational needs.
- Overcome the barriers that may exist in school.
- Increase the potential for the individual to learn.
- Increase the chances of long-term success.
- Provide support and assisted technology if required.

The five areas of specific difficulty are listed in Tables 1 to 5, with details of how children may present in the classroom and the implications for achievement.

Table 1 Dyslexia

Dyslexia	May present with	May lead to difficulties such as
Reading	Poor reading skills	Avoidance of certain situations
Spelling	Difficulty reading aloud	Not answering confidently
Recording	Need to reread unfamiliar passages	Failing in test/examination situations (especially where speed is an element)
	Difficulty note-taking at speed	Guessing information or instructions to cover up deficits
	Errors in understanding information	Perceived over- or lack of confidence
	Difficulty writing with meaning	Taking down wrong information
	Difficulty understanding new or unfamiliar materials	Not being able to take notes down at speed
	Problems reading at speed	Misunderstanding directions
	Spelling errors	Low self-esteem or lack of confidence
	Difficulty separating words into syllables (e.g. e-le-phant)	
	Difficulty telling the difference between similar sounding words (e.g. tan and ton)	

Table 2 Dyscalculia

Dyscalculia	May present with difficulties	May lead to difficulties such as
Number difficulties	Remembering sequences of numbers	Difficulty remembering telephone numbers
	Conceptualising shapes	Difficulties with geometry/abstract concepts
	Doing calculations	Getting sums wrong as a consequence
	Managing money	Managing money/calculating change
	Orientation	Copying down wrong information
	Abstract number concepts	Needing repeated explanation in different formats
	Rotating shapes	Needing help to see changes in shape or rotation
	Learning times tables	Needing to see how numbers build up
	Lining up numbers	Calculations under time pressure
	Difficulties with the language of mathematics	Confusion over terminology

Table 3 ADHD

Attention Deficit Hyperactivity Disorder (ADHD)	May present as	May lead to difficulties such as
Hyperactivity	Fidgety Jumping up and down, wanting to move around – inability to keep still	Completing or staying on task
Impulsive (e.g. answering out of turn, actions)	Topic shift or switching from task to task	Difficulty: listening to a lesson for a length of time, sitting in assembly quietly, queuing quietly in line
Attention to detail and to others	Impulsive behaviour	Difficulty learning from past experiences – repeats same mistakes
Concentration difficulties	Hyper/hypo-concentration	Difficulty staying on task Difficulty moving from task to task – may concentrate on a computer game but finds it hard to switch to others
Distractibility	Angry outbursts Frustration Risk-taking behaviour	Being excluded Getting into trouble May do impulsive acts without thinking of the consequences
Oppositional behaviour	Negative behaviour	Being excluded from school or by peers

Table 4 DCD

Developmental Co-ordination Disorder (DCD)	May have difficulties with	May present with
Fine movements	Small movements with accuracy and at speed	Difficulty dressing and undressing at speed
		Difficulty with handwriting, writing down
Big movements	Running, jumping, throwing activities	Avoidance of sporting activities
Orientation	Spatial awareness – knocking into things and people	Messy work at speed
Timing	Social integration – being aware of social rules	Difficulty doing fiddly tasks under time pressure
Smooth movements	Organisational difficulties	Difficulty undertaking a number of tasks at once
Accuracy of movements	Handwriting/recording difficulties	Turning up late or very early for class
Planning and organising sequences of movements (dyspraxia)	Making friends and keeping them	Writing short pieces
	Difficulties undertaking complex tasks	Need repeated help to carry out instructions
	Skills to time Difficulties with ball games	Slower to complete work Avoid team games
Balance	Difficulty with balancing tasks	Opting-out behaviours Late riding a bike

Table 5 Asperger

Asperger's syndrome	May have difficulties with	May present with
A severe and sustained impairment in social interaction	Not understanding the implied rules	Bad at jokes, laughing too long or not understanding
Affects socialisation in all/most situations	Poor at adapting to new circumstances	Interrupting and talking too long about one topic
Results in the individual lacking adaptability and flexibility, especially in new situations	Socially isolated from peers	Standing too close or too far from someone when talking
Increased risk of depression, suicidal ideation, and explosive temper compared with the normal population	Depth, but not breadth, of knowledge	Inappropriate comments and poor recovery from a situation, boring conversation
May have restricted and repetitive patterns of behaviour, interests and activities	Difficulty being empathic to others	Leaving a situation abruptly
Lack of empathy – little or no ability to read others' feelings and feedback of own feelings	Sensitive to noisy environment	Not picking up on idioms
May be hypo/ hyper-sensitive to sound and touch	Avoids working in groups and finds this stressful Being aware of picking up social cues such as dressing appropriately to fit in with peer group	Seen as having different hobbies to peers Formal speech, formal dress – not like peers

chapter 3

MEETING THEIR NEEDS: WHAT ARE REASONABLE ADJUSTMENTS?

GENERAL ADJUSTMENTS

DIFFICULTIES

GENERAL ADJUSTMENTS

In order to consider an inclusive approach, schools can make some general adjustments.

Consider offering the following:

- Printed sheets in different font sizes, on different coloured paper
- Raised lined paper for writing
- Access to information – such as homework assignments – on a school intranet system
- Information on audiotape (the child could record it during the lesson and copies could then be made for future use)
- Photocopied sheets of class notes
- Homework written down on a take-away sheet for the end of the lesson
- Access to IT for recording (e.g. laptops, pocket PCs, IT suite, Dana Alpha Smart)
- A choice of scissors for all children to choose (e.g. left, right, long looped)
- Different pens and pencils for all children to choose – with pencil grips and other aids
- A buddy system to take notes – using carbon paper, and at times of vulnerability (e.g. playtime, lunchtime)
- Constructing a list of appropriate abbreviations, acronyms and subject-specific vocabulary for subject areas
- Frequently used words entered into auto text or use predictive software on PCs
- School rules given to all children (consider both implicit and explicit rules and check for understanding by the children)
- Giving both verbal and written instructions and breaking them down into chunks
- To-do lists to help the child see what is to be done and in what order of priority
- A summary of salient points at the beginning and the end of a class
- Providing a clear outline of class aims and set objectives
- Checking understanding of individual learning techniques

- Prior agreement with pupils to read aloud or write on the board, and devise a prearranged 'cue' to help the child know when he or she may be asked to speak
- Using flow charts, mind maps, charts, pictures and diagrams to clarify instead of just linear notes
- Allowing breaks if required – and building in movement during the lesson every 15 minutes
- Being aware of visual or auditory deficits and teaching to all modalities (e.g. seeing, hearing, doing)
- Giving out timetable of expected work in advance and making copies available in a central location
- Ensuring there is appropriate seating and lighting – could alternative-height chairs and tables be made available for those children with postural difficulties?
- Access to angle boards
- Allowing access to drinks and toilets when required
- Making asking for help easy
- Adapting the PE curriculum with choices around movement activities that do not **have** to include ball skills and team games. Alternatives could be walking, running, swimming or smaller group activities
- Providing regular, constructive feedback

DIFFICULTIES

In addition to the general points listed above, consideration of the particular needs of individuals can significantly improve their access to the curriculum and feelings of security and well-being. Tables 6 to 14 list some adjustments which can reasonably be made for pupils with sensory impairments and those with difficulties in the following areas:

- Social and communication skills
- Co-ordination
- Time concepts
- Concentration
- Writing
- Reading
- Life skills

Table 6 Reasonable adjustments for pupils with auditory impairment

Types of difficulties	Pupils may present with	Adjustments
Discrimination	Confusion and lack of understanding when given oral instructions	Need instructions written down
Perception	Difficulties in taking notes from oral information (e.g. instructions in class such as homework)	Provide written notes before discussion in groups
Hearing difficulties – acuity	Difficulties with learning or repeating a sequence stated orally (e.g. rules or use of equipment)	After discussions or verbal instructions give a written summary
	Limited attention span and focus	Review information at the beginning and the end of a class
		Have a list of keywords or a glossary available associated with the subject
		Build up a spelling list of words most often misspelled
		Use auto text and auto correct on word-processing packages if PCs are being used
	Sensitivity to sound and/or difficulty filtering sound	A quiet work area helps
	Difficulty with concentration in a noisy setting	Partitions may sometimes be useful – away from other children
		Use ear plugs or personal stereos to cut out peripheral sound
	Feelings of anxiety in noisy settings such as assembly, lunchtimes, playground	Don't have the child sat in a thoroughfare
		Try to seat the child in a corner or opposite a wall

Table 7 Reasonable adjustments for pupils with visual impairment

Types of difficulties	Pupils may present with	Adjustments
Visual acuity	Blurred vision when reading, rubbing eyes	Transparent coloured overlays or glasses may reduce glare when reading for some people
Visual perception	Tiredness or fatigue after close work	Use buff or pastel paper to write on to reduce 'bounce'
Visual sequential memory	Headaches, eye strain or nausea when reading	Change background colours on PC
	Excessive blinking	Use a finger or ruler to help track along lines when reading
	Short working and attention span	Occlude the non-relevant text so information isn't too busy – a cardboard strip with a window cut out can help, or a ruler under the key words to be read
	Poor concentration and distractibility	Use a Dictaphone or tape recorder to take down information
	Tilting head/covering an eye	Read in natural light or with a muted bulb, avoid glaring light
	Misaligned digits in number columns	Sit with the reading book or writing material at a 45° angle – use an angle board to gain a better position
	Problems keeping place when reading	Take regular breaks
	Need for a finger or marker to keep place	Read away from distraction, so the child can focus and concentrate – a quiet room. Use reading software on the computer such as text-to-speech software
	Tendency to skip lines	Ask for verbal instructions rather than written ones
	Excessive head movements while reading	Check the child's vision – they may need to wear glasses to correct difficulties, or have a treatment for a squint

Table 7 Reasonable adjustments for pupils with visual impairment (continued)

Types of difficulties	Pupils may present with	Adjustments
	Lack of comprehension while reading	Use a voice reminder on a key fob
	Slow reading speed	Highlight key information in different colours
	Letter or number reversal or omission	Read in pairs
	Difficulty in retaining shape/whole words	Use computer software support like a reading pen (e.g. Quicktionary) or a text-to-speech package (e.g. SpeakOut)
	Inability to visualise whole words	Discuss information that is being learned in small groups, with other children feeding back to each other the key points
	Bad letter formation and recognition	Writing difficulties need to have a specific approach; check if the child has the pre-writing skills

Table 8 Reasonable adjustments for pupils with social and communication difficulties

Types of difficulties	May present as	Adjustments
Difficulty with conversations and discussions, especially in a group setting	Under extreme stress; there may be problems with emotional outbursts, irrational or irritable behaviour	Give clear instructions and check back understanding
Difficulty in adapting to new or unpredictable situations	Problems with lack of personal space – gets too close to others and is not aware of impact	Explain rules of the classroom – obvious and less obvious
Difficulty remembering instructions	Sensitivity to high levels of noise, light or extremes of temperature	Explain to other teachers why the child may behave in this way
Problems with teamwork	Difficulty with concentration	Create a system where the child can have 'time out' if getting stressed by a situation
Difficulty in picking up on non-verbal signs in others – can therefore appear tactless	Difficulty listening to others	Try to plan for change as far as possible (e.g. use timetables to cross off days to an outing). Point out conventions of dress and so on
Difficulty adapting to sudden change	Over-sensitivity or under-sensitivity to touch (e.g. dislike of being touched)	Visual reminders of actions to be done can reduce stress
	Difficulty with understanding humour and sarcasm	Be aware of this and moderate its use appropriately
	Interrupting others' conversation or breaking off suddenly and moving away	Work on social frameworks for particular settings so that the child has an idea of how to behave
	Not understanding the rules of a game	Consider quiet setting to reduce noise overload
	Misunderstanding idioms such as 'come straight to the front of the class' and then walking across all the desks to get there	Avoid idiomatic speech as far as possible

Table 9 Reasonable adjustments for pupils with co-ordination difficulties

Types of difficulties	May present as	Adjustments
General movement and posture	Backache	Ergonomic assessment of seating requirements. Seat and table height should be considered
		May need seating wedge, angle board to work from
Multi-tasking	Difficulties undertaking a series of tasks at once	Needs 'to-do lists' – even three points to tick off at a time
Tasks requiring fine motor co-ordination (e.g. handwriting)	Difficulties with tasks under time pressure	Consider other tools for writing. Try out different pen grips to see which the child likes best
Use of tools requiring accuracy or speed and fine movements such as rulers, compasses, scissors	Losing papers, possessions, not completing homework	May need working space marked out. May need filing system – help with tray or desk
Organisational difficulties	Untidy desk	Needs 'to-do lists' – even three points to tick off at a time
Difficulty with time concepts	Late for school or completing tasks in school	Encourage the child to wear a watch with a buzzer or vibrating action
Self-organisation	Difficulty making and keeping friends	Use texting or e-mail as an alternative means of communicating to friends. Teach key rules for social skills (e.g. turn-taking, starting and ending a conversation)
	Lose locker keys	May need adapted storage with different locking system, spare keys, conveniently placed lockers in school
	Withdrawn, low self-esteem	Need buddy or classroom assistant to plan work
	Difficulty trying out new tasks	Require greater time to understand and complete tasks, need to grade the activity, model what is required, and then give feedback
	Difficulty with specific machinery/tools (e.g. in chemistry)	May need adapted tools (such as in chemistry) or may need to alter position to undertake tasks
	Slower to learn to type	Teach keyboard skills, but don't worry too much about hand position

Table 9 Reasonable adjustments for pupils with co-ordination difficulties (continued)

Types of difficulties	May present as	Adjustments
	Writing slow	Use photocopied sheets and allow the child to add to them in class
		Use of audiotaping in class lessons
		Create templates for essays with use of colour coding
		Use timetable to plan out actions
	New skills slower to acquire than others	Practising skills will improve performance
		Having notes or reading matter before the lesson
Difficulty with ball skills	balance	Practise skills to improve shoulder and hip stability (e.g. crawling games)
	movement	Show the child what is expected and then get feedback on how he or she thinks they have done and what could be improved
	catching	Try with larger and slower moving balls first and allow the child to catch and throw in a variety of positions
	throwing	Give the child a clear and achievable target and see success before moving on to harder tasks
	team games	Consider other games (e.g. swimming, table tennis, running) instead
	running	See if the child can run straight before attempting more complex activities such as obstacle courses
	avoids PE and Sports Days	Consider alternative sports days where the child's skills will not be highlighted among their peers

Table 10 Reasonable adjustments for pupils with poor understanding of time

Types of difficulties	May present as	Adjustments
Not understanding time passing	Not wearing a watch, not realising that the lesson is nearly over	Use of alarms – egg timers for visual reinforcement of time passing
Not being able to tell the time	Too early or too late for class/school	Watch with vibratory mode such as 'Watch Minder'
Failure to complete tasks in time	Misses questions or concentrates on only the first one when in an exam situation	Use of mobile phone with reminder (out of school); extra time considerations in exams and a time prompter
	Forgetting homework deadlines	Use of to-do list/calendars. Someone in class to record homework and check books into bag
	Letting down friends and peers	Awareness of others in the classroom – teach class rules – the obvious and less obvious ones
	Tends to talk about time as 'It is 7.16' rather than about a quarter-past seven	Use analogue rather than digital to show the child time 'passing by'
		Buffer time built into the planning of a task
		Teach the child to break down work into reasonable chunks
		Help with organisational strategies to maximise time
		Encourage understanding of regular events (e.g. time taken to get to school every day; walk to the shops), to build an understanding of simple concepts

Table 11 Reasonable adjustments for pupils with poor concentration skills

Types of difficulties	May present as	Adjustments
Difficulty staying on task	Interrupts others	Quiet setting – use lavender smells and calming music to allow the child to learn strategies for calming
Easily distracted by noise or other people	Fidgety – tapping, pen-chewing, talking to other children	Allow the child to face the wall at times or place him or her away from main thoroughfare
Difficulty keeping focused	Misplaces information	Use of headphones or ear plugs to reduce background noise
Making careless mistakes	Forgets to complete tasks, homework lost or forgotten	Task-oriented – use of checklist, and check books in bag, homework written down
Difficulty when following a series of instructions verbally or written down	Moves around the classroom setting	Classroom assistant to keep the child on task
Difficulty keeping self and work organised	Difficulty getting to grips with an activity/piece of work	Learn some calming techniques – allow the child to move at set times
Difficulty completing tasks	Moves from one piece of work to another	Break down the work into short chunks with outcomes mapped out so the child can see where he or she has reached Allow others to tell the child if he or she is interrupting them to become more self-aware

Table 12 Reasonable adjustments for pupils with reading and writing difficulties

Types of difficulties	May present as	Adjustments
De-coding	Not wanting to read aloud	Check knowledge of alphabet and phonics
		Use large text/big pictures
	Reluctance to read alone	Read in partnership with the child
		Try paired reading
		Phoneme rules can help some children
		Label common items around the child
	Difficulty learning the alphabet	Show how sentences are broken down into words
	Poor link between letters and words	Use multi-sensory techniques to allow children to feel the words as well as hearing and seeing them
	Reading without understanding	Select appropriate books, with picture cues; check understanding regularly; explain new words
	Difficulty with creative writing	Allow for plenty of talking time so that ideas can develop; use word banks
	Slow at reading and lacking in confidence	Help children learn to read fluently by requiring them to read new stories and reread old stories every day
	Verbally able	Look to see if motor tasks are difficult (e.g. writing tasks)
	Spelling errors in a test situation	The child may need more time to process and may need words repeated several times in a test situation
Difficulty with recording at speed	Untidy work	Use of computer for recording written work
Difficulty being neat	Illegible work	Use of photocopied sheets
Posture when sitting	Avoids recording information	Annotate notes or have a scribe for note-taking

Table 12 Reasonable adjustments for pupils with reading and writing difficulties (continued)

Types of difficulties	May present as	Adjustments
Difficulty with pen control	Pieces of written work are shorter than those of peers	Use of ICT (speech-to-text) to record, use tape recorder, dictate
	Errors in recording information	Consider presenting work in typed format
	Not being able to read own notes after recording	Don't tell the child off for lacking 'neatness' – praise the effort he or she has made
Postural difficulties	Lying across desk	Use of angled board and correct seating, and desk height needs to be checked
	Hand aches after use	Allow the child to annotate notes rather than having to write everything
	Backache	Use of seating wedge, and make sure feet on floor and desk at waist height
Control	Writing above and below the lines	Raised lined paper and markers showing the start and end of a line may help

Table 13 Reasonable adjustments for pupils with underdeveloped life skills

Types of difficulties	May present as	Adjustments
Dressing	Slower with buttons and shoe laces	Use Velcro fastenings, elastic shoelaces. Give additional time at the start and end of lessons
Using cutlery (e.g. knife and fork)	Eating fast foods, ready prepared snacks	Use special cutlery (such as 'Caring cutlery'), and make sure the individual is stable when eating and preparing foods
Self-care	Losing possessions and disorganised	Label drawers, timetables and provide to-do lists
Forget to do basic tasks	Teeth left unwashed, poor personal hygiene	Reminders in bathroom and bedroom (e.g. corkboard with timetables posted up)
Difficulty wiping bottom	Smelly, dirty	Wet wipes, handle to hold on to in bathroom, list of things to do in bathroom as a reminder
Difficulty planning what order to do tasks	Disorganised and messy at school and at home	Easy-to-see calendar, use phone alarm to remind of events, egg timer to visually see time passing, baskets to organise items separately (e.g. underwear in the bedroom)
	Help with planning time and mentoring through tasks	Use of classroom assistant to help with planning and follow-up on decisions
Difficulty coping with increasing numbers of tasks		Break tasks in to small chunks and tick off as completed

Table 14 Reasonable adjustments for pupils who struggle to cope in the classroom setting

Types of difficulties	May present as	Adjustments
Cannot settle down to tasks	Fall off chair, fidget, not balanced properly, not concentrating	Adjustable chair, desk, angle board, wrist guard, regular breaks Use book rest for work or upturned A4 file Exercise at lunchtime
Difficulty with keyboard skills	Slow, errors in recording	Speech-to-text, keyboard awareness – not worrying too much about finger position
Recording	Difficult-to-read notes	Type, try using speech-to-text ICT packages
Visual disturbance	Blurring, headaches	Screen cover, breaks for other activities, check eyesight
Timing issues	Late for meetings	Alarm on Outlook, alarm on phone, timer, 'Watch Minder' or other watches set to vibrate setting
Difficulty using some tools	Difficulty turning the computer off and on; difficulty using tools in design and technology	Written instructions, shown and explained Practice skills slowly with additional time Work in pairs and threes to share different tasks
Spelling	Errors in written work	Franklin spell checker, spell check on computer, use of autocorrect on frequently used words
Planning timetable	Late, early, missed deadlines	Use of support assistant/teachers to help with work and to follow up on study plans
Difficulty with concentration	Check level of understanding – may become fidgety	Give short tasks and allow concentration breaks to enable child to move around Check whether child has understood task
Difficulty with multi-tasking	Slower, makes errors, gets frustrated or angry	Breakdown tasks into small chunks

1 WRITING

2 TIME MANAGEMENT

3 MATHS AND NUMBERS

4 SOCIAL INTERACTION AND COMMUNICATION SKILLS

5 BALANCE AND CO-ORDINATION

STRATEGY SHEET 1: WRITING

Consider the following:

- The position of the child in the chair – does the child flop over the desk or move around when writing?

1 Hips, knees and ankles at 90°.
2 Thighs and buttocks well supported on the chair.
3 Feet flat on a steady surface.

Figure 1 The ideal sitting position

- Has the child problems with stability – are his or her feet on the floor when working?
- Is the child able to copy shapes correctly?
- The tools the child is using and the shape of the child's hand.
- The ability of the child to form letters such as O, X, and + shapes.
- Has the child developed handedness?
- Has the child difficulties with language development – reading or spelling that could be affecting his or her handwriting?

Strategies

- Suggest the use of **carbon paper** between leaves of paper to give additional visual feedback and help reduce pressure.

- Try using 'Hands up for handwriting' activities for the whole class, as a warm-up activity before writing tasks.
- Encourage the pupils to try using a fatter barrelled pen with a dynamic section (e.g. rubber or insulated tubing) to hold on to. Using a spongy grip may well be better for them. Try out different pens for different tasks – there are many types available from retailers. *Edding* produce a number of pens which have been recommended by the Handwriting Special Interest Group, www.nha-handwriting.org.uk.
- Present activities in a multi-sensory format, i.e. 'feel it', 'see it', 'say it' (e.g. activities which offer resistance to movement such as chalking on a blackboard, chalking on carpet tiles, ribbons on sticks, shaving foam and sand). Try games that develop a mental image of what letter shapes look like (e.g. playing feely-bag games, drawing a letter on your back, mystery writing).
- Try using a letter strip on the desk. Alternatively, a letter strip may be placed on the back of a ruler or inside a book which is more discrete.
- Provide visual and tactile feedback by using a glue gun to raise lines on a page, or use glitter to make a line. Use colour highlighters for margins and lines.

STRATEGY SHEET 2: TIME MANAGEMENT

Strategies

- Encourage the children to wear a watch and check that they know how to read it.

- Use egg timers of different sizes so the children can see time passing.

- Practise set times (e.g. five minutes, ten minutes) and then relate this to different activities. The children can then create an inner concept of time.

- Encourage the children to estimate how long a task will take. When the task is completed check how long it actually took them to complete.

- When giving a time frame for a task, check that the children have learned how to break down time and activity into chunks.

- Play a game with the class – guess how long two minutes is and see who has difficulty with this.

- Put a timetable up on the wall of the classrom so the children can see the days going by.

STRATEGY SHEET 3: MATHS AND NUMBERS

Strategies

- Play number games with real objects so that the children can see numbers building up.

- Play the fishing game – use a rod with a magnet on the end of it and fix numbers with metal on to them, and allow the children to go fishing for numbers that add up to a certain total (e.g. 'two numbers that add up to 10').

- Ask the children to guess the number of items (e.g. paper-clips in a cup, beads in a glass). They can estimate and then check.

- Create a mathematics dictionary of terms commonly used and then the variations that may also be used (e.g. +, add, plus, in addition, sum of). Put this up on the wall to help children re-enforce their learning. Include words and phrases with confusing or double meanings (e.g. tables and tables, the square root and a square).

- Give the children a set of five numbers (e.g. 5, 7, 3, 2 and 1), and then ask a variety of questions about them (e.g. largest, smallest, sum of all of them, take away the smallest from the largest).

- Use an abacus, or other tools such as Numicon, to show the children how numbers are built up.

STRATEGY SHEET 4: SOCIAL INTERACTION AND COMMUNICATION SKILLS

Strategies

- **Musical chairs** – This game encourages all children to understand about social hierarchy. One child sits in the centre and invites others into his party. These children have to pretend to be famous people and people he knows, and they must place their chairs where he thinks they should go. The children then discuss if this is the correct position according to social hierarchy – the child in the middle, parents next, siblings next . . . strangers on the outside.

- **Wink-wink murder** – This is the old murder game where everyone sits in a circle and one child goes outside and acts as the detective. The others choose someone to be the murderer and he or she has to wink to 'murder'. Anyone 'murdered' has to 'die' dramatically. The person chosen to be the detective has to work out who the murderer is.

- **Teach a card game** – Explain the rules and pair the children off. Card games (e.g. crazy eights, snap or memory games) all teach turn-taking, rule-setting, winning and losing.

- **Emotions** – Cut out a series of photos from magazines of children and adults with different expressions. Laminate the cards. Create a set of emotion cards and let the children match the cards with the emotions. Then discuss when the children see other people experiencing these emotions, and when they feel like that themselves.

- **Moving along** – This game is the next stage and teaches the children to move in a number of ways. Each child is given an emotion card, and the others in the class have to guess what the emotion is (e.g. a choice of walking, sitting, jumping, hopping, crawling) matched with a range of emotion cards (e.g. happy, irritable, sad, irritated, angry, pleased, tired, lonely).

- **Masking it** – The children first have to make masks by painting a face on card and using elastic to attach. They then have to wear the masks while conducting a series of discussions in pairs or in threes. **The scenarios may be as follows:**

– An argument in a shop between the owner and a customer over a CD that is not working.
– Two children in a playground fighting over who has the ball
– Three people arriving at a cinema and finding that there are only two seats left
– A mother telling off her child because her or his room is messy

Other scenarios can also be made up along with these.

- **Three little words** – This game helps with communication skills and understanding non-verbal communication. Break the class into groups of two or three. Each group is given the same three words. (I use 'why', 'sorry' and 'oh'. Any three words would work.) Each has to come up with a scenario using only these three words. Actions are allowed but no words apart from the allotted three words. Other groups have to guess what each scenario is about. Then discuss with the whole class how actions and expressions tell a lot about communication and the consequences of reading the signals wrongly.
- **The sharing game** – Ask each child in the class to think about the three types of food they would want to live on for a year. As well as allowing everyone to see themselves as individuals, this opens up discussion about how similar they are. As a 'neutral' sharing activity you could pair the children off to discuss what dishes they would make and why they have chosen particular foods.

STRATEGY SHEET 5: BALANCE AND CO-ORDINATION

Strategies

Ball skills

- **Try using lighter rather than heavier balls** as they will be easier to catch (e.g. foam balls).
- **Try sitting on the floor and rolling a ball back and forth in pairs** – the child may need to have his or her back against the wall for support.
- **Try using koosh balls or wool balls** – these may be slower and easier to catch.
- **Try using a ball on elastic string** so the ball does not roll away.
- **Use balloons** – these move more slowly and give the child the opportunity to catch them.
- **Bounce the ball when throwing**, as this slows down the speed and allows time for catching.
- **Try using a bucket to catch the ball**, as this gives the child a better chance of catching than by using two hands.
- **Pair up weak and strong catchers** – this allows the strong one to aim accurately and catch difficult balls.
- **Use silk scarves** – throw these back and forth, as they move more slowly.
- **Ball with a bell** – put a bell in a balloon, as the noise will help the child recognise where the ball is coming from.
- **Change the position** – practise different throwing positions, as this is needed to gain the skills for team games.

Some traditional playground games

- **Hopscotch** – this is a good game for target practice and balance and co-ordination.
- **French skipping** – this helps the individual with rhythm and timing.
- **Two balls** – this helps with catching and throwing.
- **Mango** – this helps with listening and throwing. All players form a circle and count off (they must each remember their number). One player is chosen to be 'It' and is given a playground ball. He or she throws the

ball high into the air and calls out another player's number. Everybody runs away except for the player with that number. He or she must run to catch the ball. When he or she gets the ball, he or she calls 'Mango!' very loudly. Everybody must freeze when they hear 'Mango!'. Then the player with the ball can take two big steps towards any player and throw the ball at him or her. If that player is hit by the ball, he or she becomes 'It'. If not, the player who called 'Mango!' is 'It'.

Activities that strengthen hips and shoulders
Everyday tasks such as carrying, pushing, pulling things (e.g. boxes, blocks, play toys, wagons, carts, doll buggies) are excellent natural muscle-building activities. Put added weight into them to increase resistance.

Play equipment like climbing towers, climbing frames, wall bars, and objects to crawl through are great.

- **Play wheelbarrows** – Child holds weight on his arms while an adult or child supports his legs at the thigh. May walk a short course or pick up small, light objects. Start with short distances and increase (where space permits).
- **Row the boat** – Two children sit on the floor opposite each other, join hands and rock back and forth, trying to go as far as they can in each direction. Try to be rhythmical. They can sing 'Row, row, row the boat . . .'. Speed may be increased by suggesting windy weather and so on.
- **Climbing the mountain** – The child lies on his stomach and pushes himself backwards between two points.
- **Rafting or rowing** – The child sits on a small rug or mat (a slippery floor surface is needed). Ask the child to imagine he is on a boat and that his hands and arms are the oars. The child can propel himself backwards and forwards.
- **Walrus walk** – Lying on his stomach, child extends his arms, lifting his upper trunk and walking on arms, trunk and legs trailing behind (easier on smooth surfaces).
- **Snail walk** – With the child on all fours, place a 'shell' on his back (e.g. large beanbag or heavy blanket). Have the child walk a maze.

- **Carpet samples** – Ask the child to draw or copy patterns on to a carpet sample or doormat in chalk. Get him to rub/press as hard as possible to make the chalk disappear.
- **Crab football** – The child assumes a crab-walk position. Place a ball by his foot and ask him to kick it between two points.
- **Wrestling** – Two children (or a child and one adult) kneel up high with arms straight out and palms touching. Get them to push and resist to avoid losing their balance.

chapter 5

MAPPING SEN: A CHECKLIST

This questionnaire may be photocopied and allows the teacher to look at 'clusters' of difficulties in the areas of:

- Attention, concentration and behaviour
- Self-esteem and social communication
- Movement and co-ordination
- Co-ordination and organisation
- Literacy and recording

This allows the teacher to see if there are particular areas of difficulties that need to be looked at in greater detail.

This may be used with children aged 7 to 8 years and above.

MAPPING SEN CHECKLIST

Student's name:		
Date of birth:	Date form completed:	School year/class:
Parent/carer's name:		
Home address:		
Teacher's name:		
Headteacher:		
Special needs co-ordinator:		
Classroom assistant:		
School address:		

Reading age:	Spelling age:	
Student identified as having special needs?	YES	NO
School action/action plus/statement?		
IEP	YES	NO
List key aims:		

Attention, concentration and behaviour

	YES	NO
Timid?		
Fearful?		
Fidgety?		
Gets upset by failure?		
Withdrawn, tense?		
Answers out of turn?		
Argumentative?		
Over-eager to start an activity?		
Easily distracted visually?		
Easily distracted by noise?		
Impulsive (starts before instructions completed, impatient)?		
Not good at undertaking detailed tasks?		
Moves from subject to subject?		
Difficulty completing a task?		
Flits from subject to subject?		
Rocks on the chair, fiddles with objects?		
Over-focused on some tasks – difficult to switch smoothly compared with peers?		

Self-esteem and social communication

	YES	NO
Appears to have lower self-esteem than peers?		
Bullied?		
Difficulty managing and maintaining relationships?		
Does not adjust behaviour to demands of particular social situations?		
Avoids interaction with peers at break and lunchtimes?		
Has fewer friends than peers?		
Difficulty organising thoughts into sentences?		
Difficulty understanding the meaning of jokes?		
Misinterprets instructions at times?		
Difficulty adjusting to demands of differing social situations?		
Asks for questions to be repeated more than do peers?		
Lacks insight into problems?		
Has difficulty with speech sounds?		

Movement and co-ordination

	1 (weak)	2	3	4	5 (excellent)
Balance					
Swimming					
Ball team games					
Gym/PE apparatus					
Exercise tolerance					
Ball skills					

Comments:

Co-ordination and organisation

	YES	NO
Has difficulty using equipment or tools (e.g. rulers), or in science lessons?		
Appears clumsy or more poorly co-ordinated than peers?		
Work deteriorates throughout the day?		
Tires more easily than peers?		
Demonstrates poor posture when sitting?		
Misjudges/spills/knocks things over excessively?		
Has problems maintaining posture when standing?		
Becomes fidgety when sitting down?		
Finds difficulty catching/throwing/kicking?		
Uses PE equipment with difficulty?		
Tends to bump into doorways and tables excessively?		
Needs a reminder to take homework books home?		
Needs help managing clothes to change for PE/games?		
Needs additional time to complete tasks?		
Finds it difficult to manage own personal toilet/hygiene?		
Overreacts to unexpected touch?		

	YES	NO
Needs assistance to care for own belongings and personal items?		
Needs help to prioritise work?		
Experiences difficulties spacing work appropriately for writing?		
Continually forgets equipment/homework?		
Has better presentation skills and productivity when using ICT?		

Literacy and recording

	YES	NO
Has poor letter formation?		
Displays excessive head movements when reading?		
Has inadequate spacing?		
Skips or rereads words?		
Has no preferred hand?		
Needs to use a finger to follow the print?		
Experiences difficulties/confusion with left and right concepts?		
Has difficulty copying from the board?		
Reverses letters when writing?		
Loses place on the page frequently?		
Seems to scan but not understand what he or she has read?		
Has difficulty expressing thoughts on paper?		

USEFUL ADDRESSES

ADDIS
10 Station Road
Mill Hill
London NW7 2JU
Tel: 0208 906 9068
Fax: 0208 959 0727
E-mail: info@addiss.co.uk

Afasic
2nd Floor
50-52 Great Sutton Street
London EC1V 0DJ
Tel: (administration) 0207 490 9410
Fax: 0207 251 2834
E-mail: info@afasic.org.uk
www.afasic.org.uk

BDA
The British Dyslexia Association
98 London Road
Reading RG1 5AU
Tel: 0118 966 2677
Fax: 0118 935 1927
E-mail: admin@bda-dyslexia.demon.co.uk

The Dyscovery Centre
4a Church Road
Whitchurch
Cardiff CF4 2DZ
Tel: 02920 628222
Fax: 02920 628333
E-mail: dyscoverycentre@btclick.com
www.dyscovery.co.uk

The Dyslexia Institute
Head Office
Park House
Wick Road
Egham
Surrey TW20 0HH
Tel: 01784 222300
Fax: 01784 222333
www.dyslexia-inst.org.uk

The Dyspraxia Foundation
8 West Alley
Hitchin
Herts SG5 1EG
Tel: 01462 454986
www.dyspraxiafoundation.org.uk

Network 81
1–7 Woodfield Terrace
Stansted
Essex CM24 8AJ
Helpline: 0870 770 3306
E-mail: network81@tesco.net
www.network81.co.uk

Snap Cymru
10 Coopers Yard
Curran Road
Cardiff CF10 5NB
Tel: 029 20 388776
Fax: 029 20 371876
E-mail: centraloffice@snapcymru.org

The National Autistic Society
393 City Road
London EC1V 1NG
Tel: 0207 833 2299
Fax: 0207 833 9666
E-mail: nas@nas.org.uk

YoungMinds
102–108 Clerkenwell Road
London EC1M 5SA
Tel: 0207 336 8445
www.youngminds.org.uk